Truck Plays
Four Plays from The Truck Project

Contents

An Essay

Plays

Why We Do Theater In Trucks

In 2010, we began a theater company called The Truck Project, which creates original works presented inside twenty-four foot rented box trucks. For us, the novel choice of venue has never been merely a gimmick. Nor is it a compromise we make out of financial necessity. It is part of an overall approach to theater making that we find exciting for the freedom it affords us as artists as well as producers.

To answer a few FAQs off the bat: Yes, the audience is inside the truck with us during the show. We seat up to sixteen people at a time. And no, the truck is never in motion during the show. That would be crazy. Because there is no established protocol for doing or seeing theater in a truck, we are met with questions constantly. This is the first great advantage.

People begin to interact with art when it requires them to move outside their filter of preconceptions. When people ask us about the mechanics of truck-as-theater-venue, what they're really asking is: How alien is this experience to me? Is it dangerous? Is it slapdash? Is this an experience I can trust? They are reconfiguring their expectations, and we are careful not to fill in all the blanks. It's not going too far to say that the simple act of declaring a rented truck to be a theater venue is a creative act in itself.

We like to say that an audience member's experience of the show begins before he or she buys a ticket. The Truck Project is a larger experience that contains a theatrical performance. The artwork begins when our audience first hears about us, continues through the emails we send after they purchase a ticket, is heightened by following instructions on how to meet up for the show, and extends through the post-show cocktails we invite our audience to share with us. Presenting in a truck venue necessitates that we embrace the outside world (where would we be without bars and their restrooms?), so we find ways to frame the outside world in the terms of our performance.

This blurs the lines of what is and is not part of the show, giving audiences a theatrically heightened experience of everything around them. One night during our last run, a journalist in attendance decided to interview audience members during intermission—and no one could be sure if he was a real journalist or a performer. Every night, some random occurrence will cause an audience member to half-jokingly ask, "Is this part of the show?" Whether or not we planned it, the answer is of course, "yes."

Rainy nights are invariably the most exciting for our audiences because of the added sense of adventure in finding the truck, and the added sense of intimacy once inside. The fact that we cannot shut out ambient noise, which we once considered a liability, has in practice become an asset. There is something satisfyingly secretive about being separated from the outside world while still being aware of its presence all around you.

The challenge of creating theater that interacts with the space in a compelling way is the second great advantage of our chosen venue. To answer a question we are never asked: We will probably never do a play in a truck about two people moving apartments. We prefer to explore a theatrical space that exists somewhere between reality and agreed upon fantasy. The truck is always a truck, but it always takes on an added dimension as well. It has been a vaudeville theater, a private home, a seminar room, a fishbowl, and so on. Conjuring these other worlds requires the active imagination of our audience. They are making an imaginative leap in a space not built for these worlds, making them constantly aware of the creative act they are involved in. That's the form of audience participation that fuels this project.

Another appealing aspect of this work is the freedom it affords us as producers and presenters. We can rent our venue anytime, anywhere across the country. Though we are based in Brooklyn, we—as relatively unknown theater artists—have been able to orchestrate a tour that put our work in front of audiences in cities across the United States. The venue can be opened at any hour and located wherever parking is available.

It is also a much more economically sustainable model than most conventional theater. Even with the small house size we have been able to cover costs, and even turn a profit, on ticket sales alone. All while maintaining affordable ticket prices.

There is much that can be done in a truck that cannot be done in a conventional theater—and vice versa. To answer one last FAQ: Yes, we do also work indoors. The shows we create for a truck will forever only be performed in a truck, as they'd be much different shows if we wrote them with a brick and mortar theater in mind. But working in trucks is a great primer in how to exploit the particulars of a given environment, and a great reminder that we shouldn't take theater spaces and the assumptions that come with them for granted. Conventions are great, but using them should be a choice.

Jean Ann Douglass and Eric John Meyer

(This article first appeared on HowlRound.com in June of 2014)

The Backroad Homeshow

The Backroad Homeshow was first performed with The Truck Project on a street in Park Slope, Brooklyn, in October, 2010, as part of the double bill *The Backroad Homeshow and Not Winehouse.*

Written and performed by Jean Ann Douglass

The truck is a vaudeville theater. There are peanuts and lemonades with bendy straws available in the tiny lobby. The audience passes through a fringed curtain to a theater filled with orange, wooden benches, shiny red curtains, lit with flashlights and camping lanterns. The front of the performance space is ringed with little, flickering battery-powered 'candles'. The audience is encouraged to throw their peanut shells on the floor. There is a large suitcase to one side of the stage, and a ukulele at the back.

Jean Ann comes in.

OK, so I found out that I can keep you all in here for about 23 minutes.

It has to do with Article 3 subsection B of the local fire code that pertains to theater performances in trucks.

That, and I've been doing this scientific research on truck theater and claustrophobia, and I'll be fine for about that long and won't have an anxiety attack like I did during Iceman Cometh.

Any longer and well -

So you'll be released when this goes off.

Jean Ann sets a kitchen timer for 23 minutes, sets it on the ground next to her.

I have this performance I've directed called The Backroad Homeshow.

This isn't it.

This is like the teaser trailer.

You know, how when like Harry Potter movies are about to come out, and you're in the theater about to see something else, and they just kind of show the wand, and then they -

Jean Ann hums music that sounds like something from a Harry Potter trailer, and makes sparkle fingers around her imaginary wand. This can go on for any length of time, depending on how the audience is feeling it.

-It's like that.

Because not everyone could join us on this tour, you know, not until we have the funding. I can't really pay anyone yet, so I told them they were free to take other gigs.

Jean Ann fires off a rapid list of what the dozen or so people who should be in her cast are probably doing right now. Some of it might be true. It will sound something like:
Chloë is at Rafael's birthday.
Nick is in the studio mixing some soundtrack.
Jared is editing a music video.
Tim and I had a falling out.
Eleni's in Europe.
Sarah was really hungover when I called her this morning.
Phil sometimes has a hard time finding where the truck is parked.
Anna said she was bartending her brother's party.
Meredith has a test to take at grad school.

But I'm the director! So you know, I'm really qualified to do the acts we've been developing, best I can.

OH! Before we go any further, there's an announcement I should make.

If you got the Facebook invite, you're probably expecting a reception.

It turns out you have to get to Trader Joe's pretty early to get them to donate day-old pastries and things.

But I hope everyone got peanuts! And lemonade! Does anyone need any more?

Jean Ann calls for Eric, and asks him to get more peanuts for the people who want them. If no one wants them, she really makes sure they're sure about that.

So I was reading this thing in O Magazine the other day, about how there's no such thing as luck, or lucky people, just people who take what is given to them and are able to run with it.

I say this because next month I'm pretty sure we'll be at BAM. I've been corresponding with Joe Melillo and while he hasn't gotten back to me I think my last email was really convincing, and the full show will be ready to go by next month. His assistant assures me that he gets to all of his important emails eventually, so it is but a matter of time.

So the show opens.

And there's this really plush velvet curtain. Really plush. And like so velvety I just want to make a bathrobe out of it, but I wouldn't, because it would just be so. heavy. Though now that I think of it, maybe a heavy bathrobe would be the way to go, because it would force my shoulders down , and make it harder for me to hold all this tension I've been holding.

So Eleni steps up to the mic. Out of the sunset.

She adjusts her wig, and sets her top hat just so. And then she tells some jokes to warm up the audience.

The jokes she tells are actually jokes my mother taught me. In LEAP. It was a class for all the nerdy kids. The gifted and talented. Learning for the Educationally Adept Pupil. We'd like, mummify apples. Rake out sand pits and act like archeologists.

Eleni is very good at jokes.

I can really only remember one.

So these two atoms are walking down the street. And this one atom. Bumps into another atom. And he goes, "oh my god are you okay?" And the other atom goes "no. I think I lost an electron." And he goes "Are you sure?" And he says, "Yeah, I'm positive".

A long pause for everyone to laugh. Wait for it. It might take them a while to get it, it's a smart joke. She remembers another joke.

So this mushroom walks into a bar. And he sits down at the bar and he orders a Heineken. And the bartender's like "Hey, we don't serve your kind here." And the mushroom's like "Why not, I'm a fun guy."

Do any of you know any jokes? I can use it in the show.

But you can't just tell it. This is my show. You can tell it to me in my ear and I'll repeat it for everyone to hear.

Jean Ann does this with an audience member, repeating a few words at a time. As soon as the joke is over:

And then she just like, fades off, into the sunset.

And then the curtain opens and there's Tim, and he's got his mail. And it's like, an L.L. Bean catalogue he never signed up for, and all these bills. Like his Cablevision bill, and his Verizon bill, and he's really wondering why he has so much media in his life that he has all these bills. And there's all of these things, for, for the woman who used to live there before him. Whose name was like Larmalie, and she died or something, or we think that she did, because all of the letters are from like Medicare and Medicaid and assisted living and those scooter things. And he's always writing back on them, like no, return to sender she doesn't live here anymore, but they keep coming, you know, and they're all in his bag.

And behind him is this like, this like, giant thing of cabinets. Like, orange shiny formica cabinets with like the shiny silver edging. And I found two of them at this amazing yard sale in Ohio. And I got this really talented guy to reconstruct the rest of the set's like this huge thing of cabinets.

And then the chili's done. And you can smell the chili. It's this like really special chili that's from where he grew up. And it just sort of smells like cinnamon. And like cumin. And like meat. And it just brings up all of these memories for him like his mom and this chili and being an adolescent and a pre-adolescent and pubescent boy and the total confused feeling of getting that first pubic hair and you don't know what it is but you know it's something significant, and you don't know why.

And then you can see the letter he's writing on the projection screens back here, there's a live feed of him writing this letter and the ink is just this dark, black, like inky black ink. And it's that really liquid ink. Like if you were left handed you would never use this ink because it would smear all over your hand, with the indelible - just like the memories indelibly in your hand -

But I don't want to give away too much.

So that scene's over.

And this is the first trivia section. Sarah comes out in a tutu. It's a long story, originally there was a ballet interlude here, but then we did this performance where the other ballerinas couldn't make it once, and Sarah, being the champ that she is, was all "But oh! I have these hidden secret talents I've been hiding away in secret that you don't even know about." And the first three that she told me about I was like, woah, this is a family show! So we didn't do those. But then she said that she was a Star Wars buff and I was like ooh! My nephew is named after a character in the Star Wars young adult novels! Do that!

And y'all. You can ask this girl anything. ANYTHING and she's going to know it.

As long as it's the first trilogy.

The original. You know.

Does anyone have a question?

Jean Ann waits until someone volunteers a question. She may pick on someone. They ask.

Sarah would totally know the answer to that.

Jean Ann picks up a ukulele.

So Eleni comes back out in full clown get-up and she makes balloon animals. But only for herself. And only dogs.

Which, I'm kind of a cat person myself. But I don't even think I've ever seen a balloon animal cat. Maybe because they're softer and less angular but like, I'm no balloonologist but balloons are pretty soft and round so it would seem like it would be easy.

She puts the ukulele away.

And then there's the strongwoman act.

There's a lot of glitter and Chloë's on roller skates.

And then we're at the first sing-a-long of the show. I just learned the ukulele, myself. But I also have my accordion.

11

During this next bit, Jean Ann is opening the suitcase and getting her accordion on, not without some difficulty. It is musty. Some keys might happen to fall off.

And this is a song that I learned actually, at Girl Scout camp. I used to work at this camp in Rhode Island, called Camp Cookie. And it's like, you know how, people always name things after what paid for the thing, like the Rockefeller Camp or the Feinstein School for the whatever, and so it's like the cookies… Well, you know Girl Scouts and their cookies.

I worked in the camp store selling gimp. And we used to sing this song about the Titanic. It's actually pretty messed up when you think about it now.

She sings:

Oh it was sad,
it was sad,
it was sad when the great ship went down,
to the bottom of the -
husbands, and wives, little children lost their lives,
it was sad when the great ship went down.

She waits, expecting a reaction.

I know, I know, 'not soon enough'.

You know, like when jokes are 'too soon!' after a tragedy? And this happened a while ago, so...

So, that's not the song we're going to sing. This is the song. I'm going to tell you the words first. And I'm going to sing it.

So the words are:

Speaking:
Black socks
they never get dirty
the longer you wear them
the stronger they get
sometimes
I think I should wash them
but something inside me

12

keeps saying not yet
not yet
not yet

I'm going to sing it once for you.

Jean Ann plays a few notes on the accordion, trying to sing to it and catch her note. It's woefully off. She doesn't notice, but sings the following a cappella.

Black socks
they never get dirty
the longer you wear them
the stronger they get
sometimes
I think I should wash them
but something inside me
keeps saying not yet
not yet
not yet

I'm going to keep going and just join in when you know it.

She plays a couple of notes on the accordion as she sings. Enthusiastically.

She doesn't let the audience stop singing until they've done two rounds. She plays some more notes and then abruptly waves her arms to stop them.

Okay, so I'm splitting you down the middle. It's actually a round and it's really cool it's a round. So this is group One. And this is Group A. And we're going to start with Group A. And once we get going I'm going to run over here and tell Group One when to come in.

She plays the accordion a bunch to help them find their note. She is not matching the notes she is singing. She clearly has no idea how to play this instrument.

The audience sings it in a round. Jean Ann keeps playing the accordion. After a few rounds, she indicates that they stop, and conducts them to a close.

That was awesome, you guys clearly went to Girl Scout camp.

The kitchen timer immediately goes off.
END OF PLAY

Not Winehouse

Not Winehouse was first performed with The Truck Project on a street in Park Slope, Brooklyn, in October, 2010, as part of the double bill *The Backroad Homeshow and Not Winehouse*.

Written and performed by Eric John Meyer

The audience is seated in the round on cheap folding chairs under harsh light. A chair at the open end of the truck is left empty.

AMY WINEHOUSE enters the truck, places a six-pack of Bud on the floor next to her chair, sits, and addresses the audience. It is important that the performer playing Amy do nothing to change his natural appearance, voice, accent, or inflection; i.e., he in no way impersonates the real Amy Winehouse. Also, the performer should be male.

AMY
I'm Amy Winehouse.

Spits on floor.
Back to audience.

I'll clean that up.

I've been trying really hard lately not to be like Sean Penn in the 80's where you just see a guy with a camera and you just pop his lights out, you know what I mean? Because, basically, the way I see it—those people are just doing their job, the same way I do mine. It's just what they do. It's nothing personal for them--as fuck all irritating as it can be for me, but like, what can I say? I'm the one who put myself out there and asked for it to begin with, so I can't very well turn around and say "Okay—no, no. I've had enough for today." You know? "Don't show up where I'm on vacation; don't be there at court." I mean, who wouldn't? I would if it were me. So fuck it. You know what I mean?

I don't know. I can't even tell if I'm entertaining or not anymore. This is all I've ever done, you know? This, right here--just come up on stage and fucking throw up on people. Whatever it is, just—

Makes vomit gesture with her hand.

And then people clap and cheer and go "Oh, God Amy we love you." And then someone hands me a check.

Of course, normally I do songs…I wouldn't know how to put all this into a song though because I barely even know what I'm saying anymore, you know what I mean? I just keep talking. I've

learned to just keep talking even if I don't know what I'm saying—
it's like a survival skill. It keeps those around me happy.

So, what do you know about me? I'm hot, I do drugs, I like to get
beat up…not bad, not like hospital bad but, you know, if it's love
there's got to be another side to it…I'm very entertaining, I've got
black hair, I'm a Jew. There's not much else really. I mean, I write
songs…yeah, that's about it.

I've been trying to think out in my mind all this stuff about the
difference between truth and lies. And like, I get it but I don't.
You know? It's just become so natural that when people ask me
questions I give them an answer: "Amy, are you on drugs right
now?—No." It's not so much lying as it is filling in a blank. It's
like—I might as well make someone happy. I mean, we all know
the real truth anyway. "Amy, did you sleep with anyone while I
was away?—No, of course not, why would I do that?" It's just
easier. It's easier on them and on me. And honestly, what else am I
supposed to do?…I mean, if I were to actually go back through all
the things that actually happened…well, I don't even do that with
myself.

She stands.

I'm wearing my hair up in a beehive like I do when I'm
performing. I am performing. I'm on stage and you're the
audience. You are thousands of people. And we're between songs.
And right now I'm reaching up into my hair…I'm taking a long
time, and it's becoming obvious that I'm not trying to fix my hair
or stretch my arms or anything like that. It's becoming obvious
that I'm reaching in there to get something. I've gotten it now and
I'm bringing my arms down. I've got something in my left hand.
I'm trying to hide it from you, but you know it's there and I know
that you know, but I'm pretending you don't, because for the next
few moments I'm going to have to pretend that no one is looking
at me and no one is seeing what I'm doing…and now I'm raising
my hands up to my face and putting a bump up my
nose…*sniff*…and now I'm pretending that what just happened
didn't just happen. Because all of you are still here. And because I
am here. And it would all be too mortifying if what just happened
really did just happen.

She removes one of her button down shirts, revealing another one beneath it.
She sings:

I feel a breeze through my back
I feel a breeze through my back
I try not to react
I put my hands in my pockets
It's so good to see you
But I'm feeling my toxins
So keep yourself back
Just keep yourself back

There's a bruise on my side
There's a bruise on my side
I must have fallen last night
But I don't recall slippin'
It's been far too long
Since I felt myself lifted
But I'm doing fine
I'm doing fine

Don't try to be nice
Don't try to be nice
I'm only good for a fight
And if I can be honest
When you talk polite
It just feels like a bomb threat
So just keep your advice
Just keep your advice

She moves to the table.
She cracks open a beer and drinks it for longer than is comfortable for her.
She finishes the beer.

Through the following, she compulsively buttons and unbuttons her remaining shirt.

People keep saying that Blake and I are getting divorced, but I know that's not true. It's not. We've gone through rough patches before and it's that thing where you always think it's the end and then it's not. I mean, we're in love. We're indestructible. It's like, even if we did get divorced we'd still be together. Even if we're on opposite sides of the world and he's fucking someone else and I'm fucking someone else it wouldn't make a difference. It wouldn't change anything.

She removes her second shirt, leaving herself naked from the waist up.

I cut him up pretty badly. You all saw the pictures of that, right? I'm not telling you anything you don't know…Those cameras are everywhere…But like I said: Fuck it. And I really mean it too. I don't expect other people to understand. Why should they? Our love is our own. You know what I mean? He's inside me and I'm inside him. And when I cut him, I'm cutting myself.

She picks up her shirts and holds them to herself.

He won't speak to me, and sometimes I speak to him anyway, when I'm alone. I say things like "I'm sorry, baby. Come back. You know you want to. It's excruciating without you. I'll kill myself if you don't come back. I'll do it slowly. I'll destroy myself."

She puts the shirts down and goes to the table.

He doesn't listen. He never listens to me when I talk to him like that—when he's not really there. He just stands there all invisible. Smirking at me.

She takes out a second beer and cracks it open.

I used to love that smirk, too. He used to smirk like that whenever I said something smart. It made me feel like we were meant for each other. Now he smirks like that because everything I say is so dumb; because he knows it won't work; because he deserves better than me and he knows it.

I have to rely on the bits of himself that he left inside me. I have to hope that he wants them back—that he needs them. Sometimes I worry that he didn't leave enough, or that he never really let anything in me at all.

She places the beer on the table.

I got pregnant by him once. I did it on purpose. I didn't keep it for very long, but I just wanted to really know that I had him inside me…even just for a little bit.

She puts a different shirt on.

I'm at home now, at my place in London. It's the afternoon and I'm in one of those moods where everything's fine. The boys are all downstairs. I can hear them—the boys with the cameras. I might go bring them some tea or something, hang out for a bit. I always try to get out for a bit when I'm like this, you know, when I'm good.

I do have moments when I'm sane, it's just that in the background somewhere, lurking in a corner is this thing, yeah? And I can sense it just waiting for its moment to strike. It's like, I could be having a totally normal conversation and then right in the corner of my eye, there it is, and I'm trying my best to forget that it's there. And people say "Amy, are you alright? You seem a little distracted."

And what it is--I'm really the most loving, caring, mothering person in the world, it's just that certain things get a hold of you.

She picks up the overcoat.

This is a tube top. I use it to hide.

She puts it on.
She takes out a pair of glasses.

This is my makeup. The particular make up that I wear when I'm being Amy Winehouse in big capitol letters. I call it my war paint. It's like I'm a completely different person when I put this on. Like I'm not even a person; like I'm every girl that did a guy wrong, and every girl that got her heart broken all at the same time. And best of all, when I put this on, I'm not me anymore. I'm something else entirely.

She puts the glasses on.
A microphone is brought to her.
Background music starts for Jay-Z's "Heart of the City".

First the Fat Boys break up
Now every day I wake up
Somebody got a problem with Hove
Whatup, you niggas all fed up
Cause I got a little cheddar
And my record's movin out the store?
Young fucks spitting at me
Young rappers getting at me

My nigga Big predicted this shit exactly
"More money, more problems" – gotta move carefully
Cause faggots hate when you gettin' money like athletes
Young'uns ice grillin' me
Oh – you not feelin' me?
Fine, it cost you nothing; pay me no mind
Look, I'm on my grind cousin, ain't got time for frontin'
Sensitive thugs, y'all need hugs
Damn though mans I'm just tryin' do me
If the record's two mill' I'm just tryin' move three
Get a couple chicks, get 'em to try to do E
Hopefully they'll ménage before I reach my garage
I don't want much, fuck, I drove every car
Some nice cook food, some nice clean drawers
Bird ass niggas, I don't mean to ruffle y'all
I know you're waitin' in the wing
But I'm doin' my thing
Where's the love?

Music change to "You don't know how it Feels" by Tom Petty.

Let me run with you tonight
I'll take you on a moonlight ride

There's someone I used to see
But she don't give a damn for me

But let me get to the point
Let's roll another joint
And turn the radio loud
I'm too alone to be proud

You don't know how it feels
You don't know how it feels to be me

Sound of a huge crowd cheering.
Sound cuts out.
She takes off the glasses.

Blake.

If you can bear to listen to me, I have something to tell you. I
wanted to write you a song, but it just felt wrong somehow – like I
could write you a really good love song and get you back and then

turn around and sell a million albums with it. So I didn't. Instead I wrote you a bad song…because somehow that just felt more honest.

She turns the chair around and sits on it, facing the audience.

All I want to do is get naked and keep warm
All I want to do is get naked and keep warm
Naked and warm
Naked and warm
All I want to do is get naked and keep warm

It feels so good to be pressed up against you
It feels so good to be pressed up against you
Up against you
Up against you
It feels so good to be pressed up against you

Come inside my coat and I'll show you my sadness
Come inside my coat and I'll show you my sadness
Come inside
Come inside
Come inside my coat and I'll show you my sadness

I don't really like all this attention, really. But sometimes it feels like the only way to defend myself is to give you everything before you take it from me by force—and I know you would if I tried to hold onto it—whatever it is—whatever I have.

She gets up, slamming the chair down.
She approaches the audience.

Well then take it. I'm giving it to you. Take it. I'm giving it to you.

She takes off her coat and thrusts it at a member of the audience.

Take it. I'm giving it to you. Take it.

END OF PLAY

Obfuscation

Obfuscation premiered on a street in Williamsburg, Brooklyn in May, 2014 as part of The Truck Project's double bill *Fish and Obfuscation*.

Co-Created by Jean Ann Douglass and Eric John Meyer

Written by Eric John Meyer

Characters

PAUL: Eric John Meyer

SANDY: Jean Ann Douglass

As the audience enters, they see a small table with granola bars on a plate. Next to the plate is a sign reading "FREE CONTINENTAL BREAKFAST."

Just past the table, PAUL and SANDY stand, smiling, ushering everyone to their seats, saying variations of "Welcome, please sit. Refreshing smile. Welcome. Warm." in conversational tone.

Once everyone is seated, Paul and Sandy go to their seats between potted plants, facing the audience. In front of them is a large, brown, unmarked box.

Everything Paul and Sandy say through this section is spoken with the pleasant polish of professional conference speakers.

PAUL
Welcome, everyone. My name credential is Paul sits in front of you, and next to me female is Sandy fresh scent speaks nice.

SANDY
Welcome.

PAUL
We're so happy to have you with us...did I say, have you? I meant, be here inside your thoughts.

SANDY *as if covering for Paul's flub*
Fire! Crisis! (*Polite laugh*) Everything's fine, though—am I wrong?

PAUL
I'd like to go around the friendly room and have each of you say your name—not out loud, of course.

SANDY
And if you don't have one, or you forgot to bring it with you, an extra has been provided under your seat.

Under every seat is a three-by-five card with a random name written on it.

PAUL
Communication! That is our subject today serious. How do we harness a rope around the bull of language, launching into outer space and back to stand firmly over our fathers?

SANDY
Freedom. Power. Cadillac. What do these words mean?

PAUL
Are you as happy as you could be?

SANDY
What makes a provocative question?

PAUL
Nuance.

SANDY
Calibration.

PAUL
What do these words mean?

SANDY
What do any words mean, ever?

PAUL
This is a provocative statement. Can anyone tell me why?

SANDY
No, not anyone can. But you can. Shortly.

PAUL
Today, we will teach you the secret to words that work and
phrases that do your bidding. Language is dynamic; the world is
dynamic: shifting sand over shifting sand.

SANDY
Pamphlet two, third bullet point: How to avoid lying by changing
the subject.

PAUL
Pamphlet four, first bullet point: How to revise your intentions
after a statement you made has been criticized.

SANDY
Context is everything.

PAUL
Context is everything and therefore, also, nothing.

SANDY
Pam four, bull five: How to stop telling people what *you* think and
start telling them what *they* think.

28

PAUL
Taken together, these lessons outline the secret key that is
persuasion.

SANDY
But how will we do this? Why isn't the future here yet? Who are
these people promising us things?

PAUL
Please save your questions until we teach you how to ask them.

SANDY
Pam three, bull seven: Sometimes the word that works best is
silence.

PAUL
You may have noticed the mysterious box at our feet.

SANDY
Mysterious box. What's in the box? Is it a box of pamphlets?

PAUL
Pamphlets, cassette tapes, exercise books. Except that it's so much
more than all of these. Appearing mysteriously at our doorstep to
give our lives meaning, it contains transformative answers to
intractable questions. Answers we want to chosen people share
with you today.

Sandy reaches into the box.

SANDY
Have you noticed the change in the room?

She pulls out a cassette player and places it on the coffee table.

PAUL
Cassette tape one, side one:

He presses play and a blank tape plays silence.
Sandy and Paul listen intently for some time.
When the section comes to its conclusion, Paul presses stop.

SANDY
I never get tired of hearing that.

PAUL
I learn something new every time.

SANDY
My favorite part is the food metaphor.

PAUL
Yes, me too. Some words are nourishing, some are just filler.

SANDY
Some words are spicy, like "spicy" and "anthrax."

PAUL
And that's something I just didn't pick up on the first time I heard it.

SANDY
No, me neither. The first time I heard it, I...
She seems distracted, perhaps a little distressed
My mind went in a completely other direction almost...automatically, I...
Her tone has gone completely introspective
I thought about how I just get so tired of feeling guilty all the time, like everywhere I go I stand accused of something and nobody will tell me what. And how I'm tired of being exhausted, of not being able to sleep, of always having to play catch-up with someone else's story, someone else's version of the facts. And when defending yourself only makes you look guilty, what's left? Either you submit or you play the game. And those are really just two ways of saying the same thing.

PAUL
Sandy?

SANDY
Yes?

PAUL
It's almost time for your speech. Are you ready?

SANDY
What? Yes. I'm ready. I am.

PAUL
Just try to remember what the pamphlets teach.

30

SANDY
I know what the pamphlets teach. I mean, I know their teachings.

PAUL
Hold onto the words. That's what's important. And don't let anyone change your subject.

SANDY
No. That's a conclusion I've made for sure. No one tells me what the subject is.

PAUL
Because the subject is you.

A recorded voiceover booms from speakers at either end of the truck.

VOICEOVER
The first exercise of today's session is called Speech Therapy, but of course, we mean something completely different by that. Our Speech Therapy is a modified public speaking program designed to enhance the speech-giver's overall effectiveness. And what do we mean by effectiveness?
Pause
The speaker is given two minutes to deliver a speech on any topic. The object of the speech is to persuade. When the speaker is finished, listeners give feedback on how effectively they were persuaded. Consider, for example, how likely it is that you'll half-remember something said during the speech and confuse it for one of your own thoughts.

But before giving feedback, read all of Pamphlet Three closely, and give special attention to the Rules for Productive Participation in Speech Therapy.

The recording ends.

Paul speaks while Sandy goes through a series of physical and mental preparations for the speech she is about to give. They go on for an oddly long time, shifting continually.

PAUL
Today's speaker is Sandy. She's been working on her speech for a while now, and you'll notice how that automatically gives all of us a very warm feeling toward her. We're already glad she's here to share her thoughts with us. But as soon as she starts speaking, we

need to start thinking to ourselves "What smart thing am I going to say when she's done?" So please listen closely to the Rules for Productive Participation:

(Reading)

Rule one: Don't make value judgments. This is something we sometimes do without even realizing it. For instance, if you begin your comment with the words "I liked it when you…" you've already made a judgment of her and everyone else in the room.

Rule two: Don't be complicated. Sentences that require semi-colons or commas might impress your friends, but they're only going to make the speaker lose interest—not only in what you're saying, but in you as a person.

Rule three: Do not tell the speaker what she should change about her speech. Instead, tell her a story about an imaginary world in which her speech went differently and was differently received.

Please keep these rules in mind as you consider what comments to make.

SANDY
Okay. I'm ready.

PAUL
The floor is yours.

Paul steps back.
Sandy takes speech-giving position.

SANDY
Thank you, Paul. Distinguished guests, thank you for this chance to address you on the important topic to which I am about to something…*(checks notes)*…Does anyone know the story of the Horse in the China Shop? It's a really great story: A horse walks into a china shop and the clerk says "Please, please. Come right in, sir. I've mistaken you for a judge." And the Horse says nothing, because a horse is a horse, of course, of course, and therefore cannot speak. And as the horse maneuvers through the shop, knocking over vases and plates with its fluttering tail and bulging body, the clerk rushes to pick up the pieces, thinking "Oh, no! This broken bowl must be an important pronouncement on the fate of some condemned man. And these shards of plate must be incriminating evidence of political wrongdoing right here in my shop!" And so he follows the horse, revering and denouncing the

32

shattered remains of his livelihood. But the point of the story is: why was the horse there to begin with? What was it trying to buy, if anything, with its horse money? And where does it keep its horse money? And why?

PAUL
Thank you, Sandy. That was really something. We're going to open the conversation up to comments right now and, as it happens, I have a comment I would like to make: Sandy, I'd like you to imagine a world right now.

SANDY
Okay.

Sandy closes her eyes and imagines.

PAUL
It's a world where a woman much like yourself is giving a speech very similar to the one you just gave, except that in her speech, Sandy—and her name is also Sandy—in her speech, Sandy delves more into why the horse is important, specifically, why anyone listening should care about this horse. Do you see what I'm saying, Sandy? Do you see that world with me?

SANDY
I do, Paul.

PAUL
Great. Now, when you look around the room in that world, who else do you see? Is there someone like me there?

Sandy opens her eyes and looks around, sees Paul.

SANDY
Yes! Yes, there's someone just like you!

PAUL
Take a look at him closely, Sandy, because that man is also named Paul. Just like me. And something I know about him, in his alternate universe, is that he loves Sandy so much. So much. And he's afraid every day of losing her. And all he wants—all Paul wants from Sandy is an acknowledgment every now and then that she loves him too. A hug or a chocolate or really any signifier of affection. He's starving for that signifier. And I just thought...I

33

just thought that that would be a good thing for you to keep in mind for your speech. Will you do that?

SANDY *hoping it's her*
Are you speaking to me or imaginary Sandy?

PAUL
I'm speaking to the woman in front of me: the one I can touch.

Paul reaches out and touches Sandy.

SANDY *flustered by his touch*
I'm sorry, I've momentarily forgotten my name.

PAUL
Sit down for a bit. Look under your chair.

Sandy sits down.

SANDY
What for?

PAUL
There's a spare name for you.

SANDY
Oh, right!
Sandy grabs the 3X5 card under her chair and reads it.
From now on, my name is "Jean Ann Douglass."

PAUL
"Jean Ann Douglass." That's very nice.

SANDY
And who are you now?

Paul sits and retrieves his 3X5 card.

PAUL
My name from now on is…"Baron von Flimflam."

SANDY
Ooohh: a Baron!

PAUL
Well, it's just a title. I don't think it really means anything.

SANDY *disappointed*
Oh.

PAUL
And that's all the time we have for listener comments. Thank you everyone.

Paul starts applauding the audience.
Sandy starts applauding.
Their applause continues as Paul speaks.

PAUL
I know what you're thinking: Why are these people applauding us for just sitting here? But the truth is, we wouldn't be here if it wasn't for you. Not only because there'd be no one to hear us speak, but because we'd have nothing to say. The truth is that you are the essence of the things we are saying back to you while our associates are busy planting listening devices in your homes. Did I really just say that? Well then, I must not have meant it literally because if that were literally happening I wouldn't just come out and say it...right?

They stop clapping.

PAUL
Anyway, I forgot what I was just saying.

SANDY
Me too.

PAUL
Some of you might think you remember what I just said, but I'm sure whatever you remember is out of context and inaccurate—unless, of course, you happen to have a recording device on you. Though when you play it back, you'll probably just hear a lot of clapping.

SANDY
Oh, I almost forgot!

PAUL
What?

SANDY
As another token of our appreciation, we will now be adding juice

boxes to the free continental breakfast—which will still be available on your way out, if you missed it on your way in.

PAUL
Right, yes! The juice boxes!

Paul fishes around inside the box, finds a juice box, and places it on the table next to the granola bars.
He returns to his seat.

SANDY
Now, on to the next lesson.

Paul takes down the Speech Therapy sign and replaces it with a sign that says Role Playing.

SANDY
Now that we've learned the basics of effective communication, it's time to put it into practice with a little role-playing exercise. Consider this common scenario: Your boss calls you into his office to ask you questions about your personal life. You need to give him the right answers or he might turn you over to the secret police. You hadn't been warned about this meeting and you have no idea what he's going to ask, and you're very nervous. If he sees that you're nervous, he'll fire you. If you successfully hide your nervousness and get all the answers right, he'll send you home early with a full day's pay.
In this exercise, I will be playing the boss and The Baron will be my employee.

Sandy puts on a false mustache.
Paul puts on a wig.
They turn their chairs to face each other and both read from pamphlets.

SANDY
Sandy, thank you for seeing me.

PAUL
Of course of course of course of course of course.

SANDY
This is nothing out of the ordinary. I just need to ask you a few routine questions.

PAUL
Anything I can do to assist the company gives me great delight.

SANDY
Could you tell me where you were on the evening of [date of show]?

PAUL
My husband Paul and I were helping his brother move apartments. We rented a truck for that purpose.

SANDY
And your husband's brother, what furniture did he need help moving?

PAUL
Chairs, two potted plants, a box of loose things.

SANDY
Nothing else?

PAUL
I can have a complete list drawn up for you.

SANDY
Do that, please.

They both flip to the next page in the pamphlet.

SANDY
And your husband, what would you say his temperament is?

PAUL
Quiet. Orderly. Patriotic.

SANDY
And if he were to receive a mysterious box at your doorstep, what do you suppose he would do with it?

PAUL
Smash it to bits, then turn it in to the police for questioning.

SANDY
And what would you do if you found the box first?

PAUL
Turn it over to my husband for smashing.

SANDY
But not questioning?

PAUL
My husband would never presume to question a smashed box.

SANDY
Do you enjoy your work here?

PAUL
With all my might.

SANDY
And you enjoy, specifically, working under me?

Paul crosses his legs, gives Sandy an alluring look.

PAUL
I do.

SANDY
And why is that?

PAUL
It would be inappropriate for me to say exactly, but I have asked my husband to grow a mustache like yours.

SANDY
That is very understandable. Thank you for your discretion. You may go home early with a full day's pay.

They remove the mustache and wig, then turn their chairs to face forward again.

PAUL
That felt good. I think Sandy did well.

SANDY
Notice how she avoided being fired and won the coveted early leave by using persuasive speech.

PAUL
That's exactly the kind of success story we want for each of you.

SANDY
I think we can all learn from her strategic use of the word mustache.

PAUL
Other words that worked for Sandy include Smash, Husband, Presume, and Police.

SANDY
Try using each of those words in a sentence.
Pause
Did it work as well for you as it did for Sandy?

PAUL
It shouldn't have, and I'll tell you why. Sandy tailored her language specifically to her boss, using information she knew about him, such as his admiration for the police, and things she's heard him say in the past, such as "mustache."

SANDY
She gathered this information in a process we call Getting to Know Your Audience and then Becoming Them.

PAUL
Now let's take a look at that same conversation again. This time, pay special attention not just to what they say to each other, but what they don't say.

They put their costumes back on and turn their chairs to face each other again.

SANDY
Sandy, thank you for seeing me.

PAUL
Of course of course of course of course of course.

SANDY
This is nothing out of the ordinary. I just need to ask you a few routine questions.

PAUL
Anything I can do to assist the company gives me great delight.

SANDY
The truth is, I've asked very little from life and even that was denied me. A nearby field, a ray of sunlight, a little bit of calm

along with a bit of bread, not to feel oppressed by the knowledge that I exist, not to demand anything from others, and not to have others demand anything from me. This was denied me, like spare change we might deny a beggar not because we're mean-hearted but because we don't feel like unbuttoning our coat.

Beat

Could you tell me where you were on the evening of [date of show]?

PAUL
My husband Paul and I were hosting an illegal language seminar. We rented a truck for that purpose.

SANDY
And your husband's brother, what furniture did he need help moving?

PAUL
Chairs, two potted plants, a box of drug paraphernalia, deviant literature, and a few other things I was asked to keep secret.

SANDY
Nothing else?

PAUL
I can have a complete list drawn up for you.

SANDY
Do that, please.

They both flip to the next page in the pamphlet.

SANDY
And your husband, what would you say his temperament is?

PAUL
Quiet. Orderly. Patriotic.

SANDY
And if he were to receive a mysterious box at your doorstep, what do you suppose he would do with it?

PAUL
Smash it to bits, then hide them for safekeeping around the apartment.

SANDY
And what would you do if you found the box first?

PAUL
Keep it, study it, disseminate its contents.

SANDY
But not smash it?

PAUL
I'm giving you the opportunity to pretend I'm telling the truth.
Am I not communicating effectively enough?

Paul crosses his legs.
Sandy takes a small bowl of chocolates out of the box and offers them to
Sandy.

SANDY
Mustache?

PAUL
With all my might.

Paul leans forward to take a chocolate and eat it.

SANDY
And you enjoy, specifically, working under me?

PAUL
I do.

SANDY
And why is that?

PAUL
Because you're like an open book with blank pages I can write my
thoughts in.

SANDY
That is very understandable. Please come back tomorrow for more
chocolate.

They turn their chairs to face forward, but keep their wig and mustache on;
they are still "in character."

PAUL
I think I did really well there.

SANDY
You did alright, but don't over-sell yourself.

PAUL
I had you eating out of the palm of my hand the whole time.

SANDY
You were afraid of me, admit it.

PAUL
Who isn't afraid of an idiot with power? You're like a monkey holding a grenade.

SANDY
You think you pulled one over on me, but what you don't know is we like to keep a little subversive element around to reinforce the vigilance of good citizens. We'll stomp you out when we feel like it.

PAUL
What you don't know is what you don't know, and I'm not about to tell you.

SANDY *a little vulnerable*
But you did mean what you said, though, right? About my mustache?

PAUL
It's compelling. I'll admit that much.

SANDY
It's your husband that's the problem. I can have him removed for the both of us.

PAUL
But what if I love him and can never express it no matter how intensely I feel it because all the words for love have been turned into poker chips by the likes of you?

SANDY
It sounds like your husband is quite a dilemma.

They kiss passionately enough that the mustache and wig are removed by the time they stop kissing.

SANDY
Paul.

PAUL
Yes Sandy?

She wants to tell him she loves him, but can't.
She reaches into the box, pulls out a tape player and presses play.
It plays fax machine sounds.
Paul presses stop.
They face forward.

VOICEOVER
Now that we've seen persuasive speech in action, let's take a look at how it's made. This section is called Getting to Know Your Audience, and Then Becoming Them. You're about to hear a series of short speeches. Each one represents a potential "audience", or person you wish to persuade. Listen closely to the things they say and don't say. Then make a note of the word or phrase you hear that best represents the speaker.

Paul and Sandy pass out pencils and three by five cards to the audience.

VOICEOVER
For this exercise, you'll want to have a pencil and a few three by five cards ready to make your notes. When the speeches are finished, we'll show you how to turn these simple notes into "words that work."

SANDY
This is where the magic sausage is made happens momentous. You've arrived at the trumpets and two beams of light are talking to you. What are they saying? What are they telling you? What is the difference between the two?

PAUL
What is the difference between the two people? What is the difference between what they're saying and what they're saying? What are these strange psychological objects called words?

SANDY
Food for thought. Keep all of that with you while we present a

43

series of characters you may wish to persuade. What words do they use? What words do they hear? Paul, you first.

PAUL *playing a character*
Hi, my name is Paul except different. I would describe myself as older than I am and more intelligent. People treat me differently than I see myself and I have a terrible allergy to bees.

SANDY
Did you catch it? Because he's already told us three words that work on him, except two of them are words he chose not to use.

PAUL
You're next.

SANDY
Hi, I'm not telling my name. It's because I don't know or trust any of you and some of you scare me a little. I have two cats.

PAUL
I have just the phrase for her, but we'll see later if any of you found others.

SANDY
Paul?

PAUL
No, no. My name is Eric John Meyer. I use all three names to seem more distinctive. My insecurity is deep and I'm losing my hair.

SANDY
My name is Baron von Flimflam. I took that name when I came to this country so that no one would know I'm one sixteenth Japanese. Have you ever noticed how the number one looks like a doorman who won't let you into a building? But what does he know about my life? I don't even want to go inside your building. I'm on my way to the park.

PAUL
Is everyone writing? Because Baron von Flimflam is ready to buy whatever you're selling.

SANDY
We're almost through. Just two more.

44

PAUL
One of them is this one. The person I'm being right now. I have a
lot of self-assurance and a full head of hair.

SANDY
And I am the last person you will ever speak to. What would you
like to say to me? Have you decided what to say to me? Or are you
just going to let it come to you in the moment like a turd that rolls
off your tongue?

PAUL
Ok, pencils down and please pass your cards and pencils to me.

Paul and Sandy collect the cards.
They stand around examining them.

SANDY
These are all really great, everyone.

PAUL
Yes, excellent work. All around.

SANDY
Bravo.

They place them in the box.
They clap for the audience again.
Sandy talks as they keep applauding.

SANDY
We're clapping for you now because it's the end of the show and
almost time to leave. In a few days, you may notice new and
different kinds of thoughts occurring to you. There is no need to
be alarmed by them. Those thoughts are yours to keep and share
with friends. About a week from then, all of your thoughts will be
different and this will seem perfectly natural to you. You'll start to
feel that your current name no longer suits you and that you need
a new one. When you reach this point, you'll discover a mysterious
box left for you somewhere. It may contain pamphlets and
cassette tapes, or surveillance equipment, or instructions on how
to build a bomb. That, too, will be natural. Take the box in, turn it
over in your mind. From there, you'll know what to do.

They stop clapping.
END OF PLAY

45

Fish

Fish was first performed on a street in Williamsburg in May, 2014, as part of The Truck Project's double bill, *Fish and Obfuscation.*

Co-Created by Jean Ann Douglass and Eric John Meyer

Written by Jean Ann Douglass

Characters

ERIC: Eric John Meyer

JEAN ANN: Jean Ann Douglass

Scene 1

We are in the home of Jean Ann & Eric. They stand a great distance apart.
A table with a fish bowl on top is between them.

ERIC
What's this?

JEAN ANN
Not what, who.

ERIC
Who is this?

JEAN ANN
He's Harvey.

ERIC
It's a fish.

JEAN ANN
Don't. He can hear you. They start understanding things before
they can communicate things.

ERIC
Fish?

JEAN ANN
No, he's a…
(thinks, catches herself)
Son. He's your son.

ERIC
Well, in no way are we prepared for a son, and especially not for a
fish. I haven't even attended a fish class. I don't even know who
offers the best fish class in this town, and where the other
important fish owners go. There's so much to learn. What do we
even DO with him? How does he eat? What sorts of things do we
have to teach him? Does he have to be potty trained? This is a
terrible thing to spring on me and I'm freaking out over here. You
should take him back to the fish store.

JEAN ANN *gaining confidence.*
You don't have a fish, you have a son. You can't take back sons.
He eats dandruff. You talk to him. He's already potty trained. Just
don't say no. We need this.

ERIC
Can't you have a son and I have a fish? Especially if it's a fish that
we're talking about, and he lives in a fish bowl? And I can return
our fish to the fish store, and you can look around and wonder
where your son went until it dawns on you that your son was a
fish and he's back at the store?

JEAN ANN
I think you should talk to him. I think Harvey will win you over.
He's so cute and you could use some male bonding. You know
what? I'm going to leave you to it.

Scene 2

We are in a blackout. Jean Ann and Eric pull flashlights out of their bags, and shine them in their own faces, as if telling a story at a campfire. They are wearing ridiculous hats that look like fish, though they wear them with sincerity. During the following, they pass out swedish fish candies to the audience.

JEAN ANN
Time passes slowly when you're a fish. It also passes quickly. Really, what I'm trying to say is that fish have an unusual relationship to time. It makes sense, sleeping as much as they do. Eating as much dandruff as they do. The perpetual motion.

ERIC
It's also worth mentioning that they don't have great spatial awareness. A fish won't really notice the difference between swimming across the Atlantic and swimming laps in a bowl. To the fish, distance is just breathing. It's passing oxygen.

JEAN ANN
Fish sleep more than cats.

ERIC
Fish have a lot of babies at once, but I still haven't figured out how they copulate.

JEAN ANN
One fish, Harvey, our fish, slumbers after we go to bed.

Eric has become Harvey. He is slumbering.

The house is still, floorboards creaking as the house settles, and Harvey floats there, there in his 30 gallon tank, tucked into the nook in the front hall, next to the stairs. He isn't missing much. Few cars roll by. The noise is mostly the muffled swishes of Eric and Jean Ann rolling over in their sleep.

There is, of course, the hum of the tank itself, filtering the water, churning the underwater waterfalls under, over, and around our hero. Our hero Harvey.

The clock ticks on, as much as digital clocks can tick.

At 4:14 am, Harvey opens his eyes, getting ready for his time, now only two minutes away. He sighs and does his fish mouth warm-up exercises.

4:15, almost there.

At 4:16 it began.

ERIC *as Harvey*
Tonight, I want to tell you about the time I died.

Scene 3

Back in their home.

ERIC
Hey. Harvey is it? You being here at all is clearly a mistake, and
I'm sorry we're wasting your time, as I have no intention of
keeping you.

I was a mistake. My dad told me. And I didn't intend to have you
either, so I guess we just found the first thing we have in common!
There you have it. Something to talk about.

silence

I don't want you to feel badly that you were a mistake. That has
nothing to do with you. You're an unfortunate byproduct. And
that's not fair, I know it's not, but it's not fair for me to give you
fish food when I don't want to give you fish food and I hardly
even know HOW to give you fish food, but there's this prescribed
order of things - and if I failed to give you fish food - then I'd be
an unfit human being who could never get a fish again, even
though I wish I didn't have a fish now.

I'm telling you this because it's an important life lesson, and I
seem to be the person in charge of giving you life lessons, which is
baffling, since I have never studied life lessons and I only know
three.

Keep your nose clean.

Absolute power corrupts absolutely.

Cry over spilled milk, if you want to. Milk is really delicious and it
shouldn't be wasted.

What's that? I can't speak your silly fish language so this is never
going to work. I'm going to go now, because there's no use talking
to a fish prior to my fish training, which I don't remotely have
time for, by the way. Best of luck with the rest of your life, Harvey.

Scene 4

JEAN ANN
Hey Harvey.

I'm glad I have you alone for a minute. Now that you've been here a while, I was hoping you could help me make a map.

I'm afraid that years from now we'll have outgrown this place and we'll live somewhere new and we'll think about what this place was like, and we'll forget a whole room ever existed. Or which cabinet held the dishes. And if I can't visit here in my mind, if I can't just close my eyes and walk to my closet and know which dress is hanging next to which…

What I'm saying is, I hope you can draw better than me. Maybe you got that from Eric.

I don't know how to do this.

It's hard, because I'm not getting any cues from you.

Should we hug? It kind of feels like we should hug.

Jean Ann tries to hug Harvey.

Does that feel better?

There's a scale of shitty to awesome, and we just hugged, and I want to know if you moved over on that scale. Either direction. I can take it.

So what I'm getting from you is that I should stop trying to touch people. OK. Maybe that's been it all along.

Thank you for your honesty, Harvey.

Scene 5

ERIC
I think Harvey is pregnant.

JEAN ANN
Why?

ERIC
He's gotten so fat lately. Pregnant fat. I feel like I can see dozens of fish babies in his stomach.

JEAN ANN
We're just over feeding him. You never enrolled in that fish class, and I think we're just feeling the effects of that decision.

ERIC
There isn't a fish class worth a damn within an hours drive, believe me, I've checked. Just quacks that want to sell magical fish or something. I joined that social club in order to meet people that could recommend a fish class, but who has the time to go and make friends at a club? I work hard and at the end of the day I want to be in my sweatpants, doing what I want. But I'm not an idiot. I know what a pregnant fish looks like.

JEAN ANN
That wasn't part of the deal.

ERIC
What?

JEAN ANN
I mean, what are we supposed to do now?

ERIC
I don't know.

JEAN ANN
If Harvey has babies, he won't need us anymore.

ERIC
How can you say that?

JEAN ANN
It's true. I'll have to learn how to make angel food cake. I'm not ready to be a support system for a support system. I won't do it. I can't.

ERIC
Do you want a hug?

JEAN ANN
No! I told you. I can't do that anymore.

Scene 6

JEAN ANN

I've been thinking about what you said, and I want you to know that I haven't touched Eric since we had that conversation. But I want to confess that I haven't been totally perfect at it. We still share a bed, and he sleeps really soundly, and sometimes at night, I will touch him, because he won't know, right? I lie there and stare at him while he is still as a stone and I can't help it, I put my hand on his back to make sure he's still breathing. And then I feel his rib cage expand and contract, and I probably shouldn't do this, but I leave my hand there. For a while. Five or six breaths, sometimes. I love that I can feel his bones, and the muscles over the bones, and the muscles sliding over the bones as they pull up and let him breathe. It's slippery and strong in there. Inhale. Exhale.

I hope it's not affecting his dreams. Is it affecting his dreams? I'd like him to be dreaming positive things about our family, and do you think if I touch him it gives him bad dreams? Hello? I can't understand what you're trying to tell me.

Jean Ann pulls out a pamphlet from her pocket. Reads.

"If your therapy fish is having a hard time communicating with you, try asking direct questions and counting the bubbles from his mouth. Five bubbles means 'yes', seven bubbles means 'no', ten bubbles means 'ask again later'. "

Jean Ann puts the pamphlet back in her pocket. Gets in close to Harvey.

Should. I. Stop. Touching. Eric's. Back. When. He. Sleeps.

She watches and waits. She pulls out the pamphlet and re-reads a bit.

It doesn't say how long I watch for. That was fifteen bubbles. Harvey, how long do I watch for? I can't hear you anymore. Harvey?

Scene 7

ERIC
Can I tell you a story? I don't know why I ask, you're a captive audience whether you like it or not.

I have this really vivid memory of being a little boy, and we had a snow day. It was a day we were supposed to go to school. School means something different for humans, and I was supposed to be at school, but it was snowing.

Oh shit. You don't know what snow is. Well.

Humans live in a world of air. You live in a world of water. There is air in your world, and water in ours, but it's not so omnipresent. Sometimes it falls from the sky. If it's really cold, it falls from the sky in soft, fluffy ice crystals, and it collects in piles and blankets and covers huge areas until humans move it, bit by bit, or the sun comes out and turns it into regular water. Except once it turns into water, it doesn't stay around us like your water. It sinks. It absorbs into the ground.

I guess snow is the closest I'll ever be to knowing what it's like to be you. To be surrounded by piles of water you need to plow through in order to move.

Hey Harvey. I started to tell you a story, because I wanted to be closer to you. But now I feel closer to you because of this other thing, so I'm going to stop talking. I'll just stop talking and we can sit and I can listen to the water in your bowl.

Scene 8

JEAN ANN
How did it go with him today?

ERIC
Great. We just sat with each other.

JEAN ANN
That's not what you're supposed to do.

ERIC
I didn't know I was supposed to do anything.

JEAN ANN
It says… *(pulling out pamphlet)* to talk at least 15 minutes a day. "For maximum healing, talk 15 minutes a day to your therapy fish."

ERIC
Therapy fish? THERAPY FISH? Our son is a therapist?

JEAN ANN
He's not our son. I bought him for us. You're supposed to talk. It's a process.

ERIC
I knew it. He looks nothing like me. And he loves talking. I never like talking. I never have, and you married me anyway. Just sitting makes me feel good.

JEAN ANN
This isn't supposed to make you feel good. It's supposed to be healing for us. Healing for this bubble between us that was forged the first time we touched, and is fragile and broken and is the greatest thing I'll ever be a part of. Just sitting around doesn't patch the bubble. I want the bubble to be so strong that if I'm not able to exist any more, I can just lean on the bubble and it will be strong enough that the world will still think I exist.

ERIC
Where is this bubble?

JEAN ANN
It's here.

59

ERIC
I don't see it.

JEAN ANN
If you're saying that to hurt me, I wish that you wouldn't.

ERIC
Is it a metaphorical bubble? Is that it?

JEAN ANN
It's here.

ERIC	JEAN ANN
Or a symbolic imaginary bubble?	
A freudian bubble?	No.
A simile of a relationship bubble?	
A figure of bubble speech?	No.
An old wives bubble?	
A hyperbolic bubble?	
A motivational imagery bubble?	No.
An Aesop's bubble?	
Is it something your yoga teacher told you to	
imagine?	

JEAN ANN
No.

ERIC
Is it this fish tank?

pause.

Is it this fish tank?

JEAN ANN
I think we need to take a trip.

ERIC
A trip?

JEAN ANN
It will be good for us.

Scene 9

Blackout. Fish hats. Flashlights. Eric is Harvey.

JEAN ANN
As the lights dim and motion in the house slows down to a
rustling, our hero waits and naps and waits and naps.

4:16 am is approaching. Harvey must rest. Harvey has much to
say.

The clock ticks. 4:16.

ERIC *as Harvey*
They had gone away for days. You know they're going away
because there is so much dandruff in the bowl. Way more than I
could eat in one day. You can tell how long they're going to be
gone by how cloudy the world is with food.

After some time of eating away at the piles of flakes, it started
getting colder. My world started getting thick, and thicker. It was
thickest when it was dark. When it was lighter, things would be
less viscous, and then when it got dark, it was thicker and
thicker... and thicker and thicker... and then all at once or after a
long, slow thickening, I stopped being able to swim. My air was
solid. My scales stuck to the immobile water.

And that's when I died.

Scene 10

Their home. They are returning from vacation.

JEAN ANN
My god, that air. I already miss the air.

ERIC
It was like taffy.

JEAN ANN
It was like the ocean. Because the ocean was so nearby.

ERIC
It was like popcorn and corndogs. Just inhale exhale.

JEAN ANN
Inhale exhale.

They share a moment.

Inhale exhale.

ERIC
Inhale exhale.

They share another moment. We see the vacation magic already start to wear off. They register their reality.

I feel so… So… I feel that now that we've been on a trip and we've breathed that air and I think we both feel good about… I just want to know… Would you like to hug?

JEAN ANN
Why are you asking me that? Do you like it when that happens?

ERIC
Most of the time.

JEAN ANN
I thought…

ERIC
I'd like to show you affection, and the trip was affection, but now we're no longer on the trip, so I think we should hug.

JEAN ANN
Harvey told me that my hugs make him feel worse. I don't want to do that to you.

ERIC
Fish don't like hugs. They can't hug you back. I can hug you back. I'm a man, not a fish. And even if Harvey is a brilliant therapy fish, there are some things he can't do. I can walk. I can ride a bicycle. Without training wheels, I might add. I can sit in a chair. I can make breakfast and sandwiches. I can read out loud. I can use a fork. I can use a debit card. I can buy socks. I can shave. I can throw you a birthday party and I'll even invite your friends that I like.

Jean Ann runs to him. They embrace.

JEAN ANN
It's the dead of winter here. It's like the heat turned off while we were gone.

As JEAN ANN speaks, ERIC notices the bowl.

ERIC
Oh hey Harvey! Bet you're in need of some fish food.

JEAN ANN
I bet he is!

ERIC
He's so still.

JEAN ANN
Oh. No. But he's not belly up. Is he belly up?

ERIC
No. He's top up. Maybe some food will speed him up.

ERIC shakes his head over the bowl. It doesn't sink into the water, because the water is ice.

ERIC
Oh, I see.

JEAN ANN
He moved?

ERIC
No, he's frozen. We froze our son.

Scene 11

Jean Ann is alone. We hear the sounds of ice chipping from off.

JEAN ANN
I don't think we should have anyone over for a bit. I'm too sad. I know people will start bringing casseroles any minute now, but we should put a sign on the door that they can leave them without ringing the bell, and we can set an alarm to remember to check the stoop for casseroles on a regular basis. I think if we do it every hour, none of the casseroles will go bad. But I suppose we then run the risk of running into the casserole-bringers once an hour, and that just won't do. Maybe we can tell them to not bring casseroles at all, what do you think? Of course, I don't know what we'll eat for the next few days, but we can manage. How do you get in touch with the casserole people? Are they the same people that bring the lunch meat trays, or are they at a different number?

ERIC *from off*
I don't think anyone is bringing any casseroles. At least not until the obituary comes out.

The chipping sound stops. Eric enters.

I've been dreading having to write this since you brought him home. Can you take over for a bit?

JEAN ANN
Sure.

ERIC
I want to start this.

Jean Ann leaves, we hear the sound of ice chipping again. Eric writes.

ERIC *continues*
Harvey was a good fish, a wise fish, whose life was cut short by a freezing accident. He may have seemed to you like a trained therapy fish posing as a son, but you never would have known that, if you had met him. He inspired the people around him, his family, to talk, to share, and to take vacations when they needed them. It was during one such vacation that Harvey met his untimely demise.

JEAN ANN *from off*
Honey?

ERIC
Yeah?

JEAN ANN
My arm's getting really tired, and I'm afraid I might chip too hard and injure him.

ERIC
Don't do that.

JEAN ANN
I know. I'm thinking I should heat the kettle up. That might be nicer. What do you think?

ERIC
I hadn't thought of that. I think it will be nicer. Just be careful to pour slowly.

JEAN ANN
Of course!

ERIC *back to writing*
Harvey spent every day swimming, sucking in water and fish flakes, and leaving long strings of poo. That he is no longer with us is the result of a tragic accident, and not the result of any negligence on the part of his parents, who were, at the moment of his demise, most likely discussing how happy they would be to see him when they came home, and are two swell, yet very sad, responsible adults who are currently devastated and in need of your pity. They are asking that you not send casseroles, or lunch meats, please, but donations of flowers will be accepted on an as-needed basis.

He leaves behind his mother and father, who adopted him not too long ago, but who aren't sure what they will do without him, once they chip (*stops, crosses this out. writes again, correcting himself*) melt him out of his icy grave and flush him down the toilet. It's not a hero's burial, it's the sad burial of a fish taken from us too soon. Of a fish drowned in solid water. It's the only thing I think I can do for you, Harvey, and I'm terribly sorry it's not nicer. You were so nice to me.

JEAN ANN *from off*
Ohmygod! Come here! Something's happening! Quick! Now!

Eric runs off. There is a light change. Music begins to play. Perhaps it is "Ooh Ah (Just a little bit)" by Gina G.

Harvey comes out. He is huge, most likely a puppet. As the music plays, he gives birth to a whole bunch of little fish. We are in the toilet bowl, witnessing the fish pop out around us.

There is pomp. There is circumstance. It might be a little gross, it's a birth after all.

The birth ends and there are fish everywhere. I mean, EVERYWHERE. We are exhausted. That was rough.

THE LAST SCENE

Blackout. Flashlights. Fish hats. The little fish are all around us, in piles and drifts.

JEAN ANN
Harvey is resting up, swimming while sleeping, traveling miles in his slumbers, staying in one place.

Shhh, the little fish say to each other, be quiet and let him rest. It's 4:05, don't wake him early.

They all look at Harvey expectantly, waiting for the next chapter in the story. This is their favorite time of night. The stories he can tell! Other fish tanks. Toilets. What it's like to be the only fish in a bowl.

4:11. The little fish jockey for space, pushing each other out of the way. Their tails wagging in excitement.

4:16.

ERIC *as Harvey*
And then, there you were. All of you.

And there I was.

And there we all were.

And here we are. Here we are.

END OF PLAY

The Truck Project is a co-creation of theater artists Jean Ann Douglass and Eric John Meyer. The Project premiered in 2010 with a double bill of solo performances The Backroad Homeshow and Not Winehouse, which played in Brooklyn, New York, Spartanburg, South Carolina, New Orleans, Louisiana, and Austin, Texas. The Truck Project's latest double bill of short plays Fish and Obfuscation premiered in May and June of 2014, in Brooklyn.